DATE DUE

MAR 5 '93			
MAY 19 '93			

Horses at Work

Charlotte Popescu

Batsford Academic and Educational Ltd London

Typeset by Tek-Art Ltd, London SE20
and printed in Great Britain by
R. J. Acford Ltd
Chichester, Sussex
for the publishers
Batsford Academic and Educational Ltd,
an imprint of B.T. Batsford Ltd,
4 Fitzhardinge Street
London W1H 0AH

ISBN 0 7134 4451 7

ACKNOWLEDGMENT

The Author and Publishers would like to
thank the following for their kind permission
to reproduce copyright illustrations: City of
Aberdeen, Department of Leisure and
Recreation, fig 66; BBC Hulton Picture
Library, figs 1, 3, 4, 5, 10, 11, 12, 22, 42;
Imperial War Museum, figs 45, 46, 47;
Mansell Collection, figs 2, 6, 17, 28, 34;
National Coal Board (John Cornwell), fig
53; Ann Ronan Picture Library, fig 19;
Sussex Police, fig 63; John Topham Picture
Library, figs 40, 62; Josiah Wedgwood
and Sons Ltd, fig 29. Fig 16 is reproduced
by Gracious Permission of Her Majesty
The Queen. Fig 59 is the property of the
Author.

J
636,1

1. Horses

C

Contents

The Illustrations

4

1
Horses
in Early Times

Prehistoric man valued horses for their flesh and hides, cavemen painted pictures of them on the walls of their caves, and Nomads travelled with herds of mares which they kept for their milk. However, for at least 4,000 years man has used horses for war, hunting, sports and for transporting himself or goods from one place to another.

The First Uses of the Horse

Horses were domesticated after cattle, sheep, pigs and donkeys and, evidently, early on, horses, which were much smaller than now, seemed less useful. When the horse was

1 Cave painting of a horse which is superimposed on a deer.

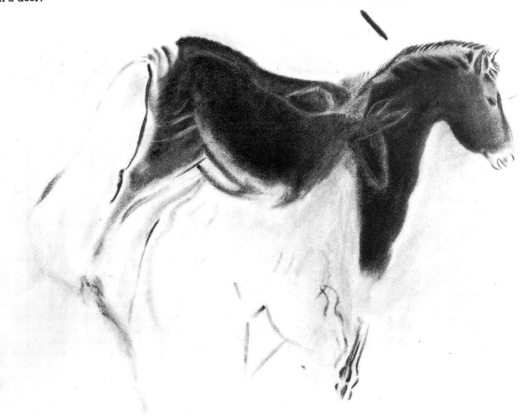

domesticated, it was first used for driving purposes. The Aryans, living in Mesopotamia, used horses to drive their war chariots against the enemy, and the Babylonians were using horses and chariots in 2000 BC. This new use of the chariot in war quickly spread until, by about 1750 BC, most tribes of Western Asia and the Egyptians were using them. It was probably not until war chariots came into being that the horse, with its speed and agility, was recognized as the most useful drawer of anything on wheels. Before then, oxen had been used as the pullers and mules as pack animals. They continued to be used as such, but horses were also gradually used for these jobs. By 1500 BC the chariot had become heavier and required more

horses to pull it. The Assyrians used heavy war chariots which carried up to four soldiers into war. However, it was difficult to drive these chariots up and down slopes and, relatively soon, chariots were relegated to use for racing only.

The horses that first drew these chariots were small, but gradually became larger, with selective breeding, until they were big enough to carry men, and warriors found themselves more effective mounted on their horses. So, from about 1000 BC, we have evidence that the Babylonians were riding into battle and, slowly, different races formed cavalries.

The Greeks

Amongst the Greeks, riding also came into practice later than driving. In the Heroic Age, around 1000 BC, battles were fought in

2 "Seven against Thebes" from a Corinthian vase, 575-550 BC. Greek warriors leave in their chariots in the expedition against the city of Thebes.

▼

3 Alexander the Great tames his horse Bucephalus.

chariots by the heroes, and by the rest of the army on foot. Chariots were also used for long journeys, but it was for racing that they were primarily used. These races were run at the Greek Olympic Games as early as 700 BC. Races were introduced for ridden horses in the 600s. It was not until the Persians had begun to use a cavalry in their armies in the 500s that the Greeks followed their example. The Greek cavalry, however, was never really an important part of the army or greatly successful. The cavalry was small, since few men could afford to supply themselves with horses.

Xenophon, the famous Greek commander and historian, wrote about horses and we learn much about riding in Grecian times from his work on horsemanship. In this book Xenophon covers, amongst other things, stable management, equitation and the cavalry. There were no saddles or stirrups used as yet. The cavalry used saddle cloths and very severe bits at this time; also spurs. The Greeks were the first to ride

to hounds and Xenophon also wrote a book on hunting. The Libyans and Egyptians had hunted, but had pursued their quarry by chariot. Xenophon saw hunting as the best training for war and, indeed, in the ancient world young military leaders were chosen from those who showed initiative and courage out hunting.

It was in the fourth century BC, under Philip of Macedon and Alexander the Great, that a more sophisticated use of cavalry was developed. King Philip originated the cavalry charge, and the cavalry, which before had fought in disarray, learnt to fight in a more orderly fashion. His son, Alexander the Great, was a great cavalry leader and won his famous stallion, Bucephalus, from his father. The horse was unridable, but Alexander noticed that he was being frightened by his own shadow. So he turned the horse toward the sun and mounting, rode him successfully. Philip then presented Bucephalus to Alexander. Alexander was also a keen hunter and commanded Aristotle to write a treatise on the chase.

The Romans

The Romans, fond of chariot races like the Greeks, held these in the Circus Maximus a

4   A portion from the largest mosaic preserved from classical antiquity. It formerly covered the floor of a hall in a house at Pompei. War wages between the Persians and Macedonians. Darius turns in flight and Alexander the Great starts after him.

▼

5　Chariot racing takes place in the Circus Maximus at Rome.

Rome. The drivers were usually slaves and the chariots started in a slanting line and were raced round an oval-shaped track. In the ridden races each rider was given two mounts and leapt from one to the other. The Romans did not use chariots on the battlefield.

Horses were important in Roman wars, but were used mainly for hauling, or as a cavalry for light skirmishing — the infantry doing most of the hard fighting. Caesar landed in Britain in 55 BC with a strong cavalry force and won several battles. The Britons, without cavalry at this time, could only use infantry or chariots. Boadicea, the famous British queen, used her horses and chariots (so we hear from Tacitus) to attack the Romans, using a chariot with knives embedded in the wheels.

The Romans also used their horses as pack animals, an essential form of commercial transport in Imperial times. Otherwise, they were used primarily for hunting boars, which were killed by javelins thrown by the riders.

The Romans are also credited with the invention of the horse-shoe.

Attila the Hun

With the fall of the Roman Empire, the Goths and Huns gained superiority. Attila the Hun was a great master of military horse strategy at this time, and boasted that, wherever his horse stepped, the grass would never grow again. He was a keen horseman and spent a lot of time in the saddle, even eating while on his horse. It was under Attila that the Huns won battles against the Romans in the fifth century AD.

9

The Dark Ages

Little is known about the development of the cavalry and use of the horse during the next few centuries, known as the Dark Ages. The stirrup was invented around 700. In Europe soldiers grew heavier with the increased weight and size of their armour. So stronger and larger horses were bred to carry them.

The idea of chivalry and knighthood probably developed with the rise of the Franks, the chief tribe of Germany in the 500s. The legendary King Arthur and his knights of the Round Table were living in Britain around the 500s, but little is known about their principles and practices of knighthood. It was not until 1066, when the Normans came to Britain, that the real concepts of chivalry began to emerge.

▲
6   The Fall of Rome. Attila and the Huns invade Rome.

Ancient Britain

To go back a little, we have evidence that during the Iron Age, from 1000 to 55 BC Britons were using horses and chariots. Horses were also probably used to pull carts. Pack ponies were used in England to transport their bales of cloth, in the same way as they were used to transport goods all over the Roman Empire. The Romans were responsible for introducing races between mounted horses to Britain.

2
The
Middle Ages

William the Conqueror's Horses

The Bayeux Tapestry is our first valuable record showing how the Norman knights under William the Conqueror rode and fought, and the armour they wore. At this time, the knight was a cavalryman. There was no ceremony of knighthood and very little concept of chivalry. William the Conqueror invaded Britain, bringing with him his 1,000-strong heavy cavalry. There were stallions bred big to carry a knight in armour. The knights wore conical iron helms, and hauberks which were rather like night-shirts, calf-length and with half sleeves. The armour was either linked chain-mail or overlapping metal scales sewn onto leather. The knights also carried shields, sword and lances. All in all, the knights' horses probably carried about 16 stone.

7   An extract from the Bayeux Tapestry. See how small the horses are — the cavalrymen's feet are almost on the ground.

▼

8 A thirteenth-century battle scene. The knights are wearing chain-mail and early-type helmets.

The Crusades

The Saxons in England, whose horses were much smaller and were still used for hunting rather than war, were unable to withstand such an enemy. So, after the Conquest, William the Conqueror introduced his horses to Britain and during the 1100s more were imported from Europe. There is evidence from William Fitzstephen's description of Smithfield Horse Sales, that, in Henry II's reign, horses were still being imported from Europe in 1171. King John also imported horses for breeding, in an effort to improve the weight and size of the English horse.

It was the Crusaders who brought many new ideas to Britain from the East, and these included new theories on war tactics. They had lost battles against the Turks who were very fast and skilful on their horses, cunningly using false retreats to confuse the enemy, and who were also very good archers. The Crusaders learnt from the Turks to use close formation and to keep their infantry and cavalry working close together. Richard the Lion Heart led the English in the Third Crusade. A famous story tells that Saladin, the Turk, sent Richard a fine charger. Richard, being suspicious, told a groom to mount the horse which immediately bolted straight back to the Saracen camp. Saladin, ashamed, then sent Richard another horse which was better trained!

It was during the Crusades that the first horses from the East were brought to Britain. More agile and swifter than the great horses of Britain, they were at first used mainly for foraging and reconnaissance. As mentioned later, they were also bred for racing purposes.

Chivalry

Finally, in the late 1100s, the idea of chivalry came to England from France. The Crusaders played a part in this, returning from the East with all the trappings of luxury a knight could desire. Chivalry indeed transformed the life-style of the upper classes. Gentlemen were now expected to indulge in sport such as hawking, hunting and fighting in tournaments.

Tournaments

In the early Middle Ages tournaments were forbidden by Church and State (both disapproving of the cost in money and lives), but later they were allowed. At first, tournaments were simple battles fought by a number of knights, with from two to a hundred on each side. These became a part of military training — pretence battles which were rough but casual. However, by the 1200s they had changed to become organized spectacles rather than battles. Single combats were fought and judged by umpires. Each knight, as was the French practice, would choose a woman and fight in her honour. If he won he would reap his reward, and a wife was forced to commit adultery. The knights used blunted lances and the object was to knock the opponent off his horse. The victor won the loser's horse and armour. The tournaments were not only excellent training for war but exciting spec-

tacles. Ladies were keen spectators. Sometimes the tournaments were held for political purposes, for pomp and show, to impress foreign visitors with the wealth and importance of the nation, or maybe to distract the common people in times of unrest or misfortune.

By the 1300s the relevance of tournaments as military training began to disappear. The long-bow was invented and became the principal and most effective weapon, and this led to the development of a better armour called plate armour. This replaced the mail armour and was heavier. Therefore, horses had to be bred even larger. Horses also wore armour to protect them from the arrows and, since they were now carrying up to 30 stone, they were unable to

9 The later type of tournament. Note that the tilt (the barrier between the jousters) had now been introduced.

▼

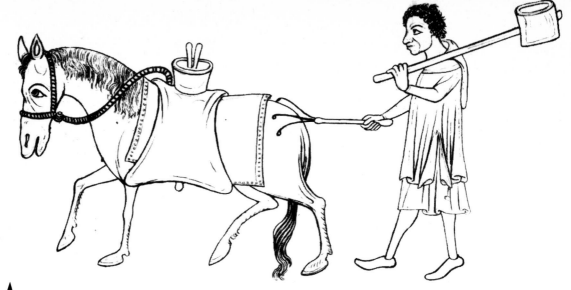

10 A very ugly man and pack pony from the Luttrell Psalter (a fourteenth-century illuminated manuscript).

move into battle at anything faster than a trot. It is said that the knights were so heavy that they had to be hoisted into the saddle by a primitive crane.

By the 1400s tournaments had become little more than sporting events. At first, to prevent the smashing of knees as horses passed close together, pads of straw were bound to the horses' chests. Then the "tilt" was invented to keep horses apart. A rope was used at first and then a firm wooden barrier.

Transport and Travel

During the Middle Ages pack ponies were used as the main means for transporting goods. Pedlars of all kinds travelled the highways, with their goods in panniers

11 Pilgrims on their way to Canterbury. The woman rides pillion — she doesn't look very safe!

12 These horses are harrowing and sowing the fields in the 1400s.

on pack horses. 220 lb was the standard pack-horse load. There were dangers, though, in travelling, from the highwaymen, armed bands of robbers, waiting to attack passers-by. Edward I passed a law against them, saying that the land at the side of the highways must be cleared so that robbers could not hide in the bushes on the verges. Another problem was the terrible condition of the tracks, which the public were obliged to repair themselves. Of course, many mounted travellers also used the roads. Ladies, in these times, rode astride, but there is evidence that a form of side-saddle was used in the 1100s. However, more often, ladies seem to have ridden pillion (i.e. the woman sat behind the man on a saddle which was attached behind the main saddle). The very rich sometimes travelled in a horse litter — rather like a sedan chair but with shafts carried by horses rather than chairmen.

Horses on the Farms

Horses in the Middle Ages were being employed on the farms. Oxen were the farmers'

early workers. They could be driven by the yoke, which could not be used on horses because it was painful on their necks. The Chinese invented the horse collar, basically a pad going round the horse's neck, and this collar was adopted in Britain in the early Middle Ages by farmers who used horses for ploughing. These were often brood mares, as stallions were bred for war. The mares also pulled the farm wagons. However, oxen were still considered more economic, since they could also provide meat and hides for clothing. So, although horses were gradually replacing oxen in parts of England, this process was not to be complete until at least the 1700s.

Hunting

Hunting was also an important medieval pastime. It was, of course, a major source not only of food but also of ostentation. William the Conqueror first introduced hunting as a sport to Britain. Wolves and boars were hunted, but deer-hunting was particularly popular. The deer were chased by slow

13 "Pulling the farm wagon" from the Luttrell Psalter.

▼

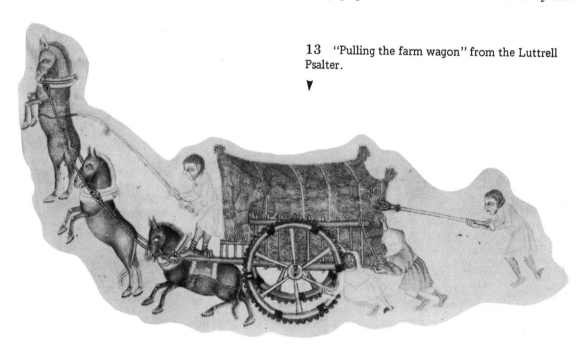

16

14 Stags were often hunted with arrows in early hunting.

hounds and by gentlemen on large slow horses. It was even then a dangerous sport. William II's death by a hunting arrow in the 1100s was the first recorded hunting accident. Hunters at this time either used hounds to pursue their quarry or used bows and arrows, shooting from the backs of their horses. Towards the 1300s hare-hunting increased in popularity but was considered less noble and produced less food for the table than the hunting of larger animals. The fox was hunted in the Middle Ages, although it remained for some time to come less popular, being regarded as an inferior animal of the chase. It was at the end of the 1300s that Richard II gave the Abbot of Peterborough permission to hunt the fox.

Early Racing

Another sport's beginnings can also be seen in the Middle Ages, namely racing. Unorganized races are known to have been held at the Smithfield Horse Sales. There is also evidence that, in Richard I's reign, knights raced for substantial prizes. Richard I owned two running horses, equites cursores, as they were called then. These were rare at this time and must have been partly of Arabian blood, imported as a result of the Crusades. John I was also said to have running horses in his stables and this shows that even in this age a distinction was made between running horses and other kinds of horses. The object of early racing was to prove the courage and skill of the horseman rather than the quality of the horse. It was not until the genesis of the thoroughbred that the quality of the horse became all-important.

3
The Tudors and Stuarts

Henry VIII

At the start of the reign of the Tudors, the English were still keen to preserve the heavy horse, the courser, that had distinguished itself in war and tournaments. Henry VIII was a keen breeder of horses and passed legislation to forbid the export of horses, and to stop stallions under 13 hands high (hh) being used for breeding. He also insisted that all men of rank should keep horses suitable for the cavalry. Henry VIII imported horses from Spain and Italy. In 1520 he met Francis I at the famous Field of the Cloth of Gold, a meeting designed to show their respective strengths. Unfortunately, it only proved the superiority of the French horses over the English. Henry VIII, however, did not make much use of his cavalry, being more concerned with building up the navy. He preferred to use horses for his favourite sport, hunting, and for tournaments, of which he was a keen supporter. He himself competed in these and his massive suit of tilting armour can be seen in the Tower of London today.

Sixteenth-Century Tournaments

The tournament of the 1500s was a purely ceremonial occasion. Further precautions were invented to ensure that the tourneys would be harmless. The pommel of the saddle now rose up as an iron shield to cover the rider's body and the saddle was equipped with special iron leg-guards and had no cantle, so that the rider could slip off the back of the horse. The idea of chivalry had died and the tournament gradually gave way to the Carousel, a sort of pageant for which the rider would dress up and cover his horse in finery. These riders took part in stately musical rides and performed feats of horsemanship in displays. Tilt-yards were still used and riders aimed their lances at rings or quintains, false heads, which swivelled and whacked the rider if hit wrongly.

Horses for War

In war, the horse was becoming less important, especially as a result of the invention of the long-bow. With this, the enemy could present a line of razor-sharp blades which a line of horses were unable to penetrate. The heavy charge of massed horsemen was abandoned and thus there was less demand for heavy horses. The invention of gunpowder meant that a cavalryman was no match for an infantryman and his musket.

During the 1600s there was a growing emphasis on the breeding of fine horses. In their stables the squires kept one or two

15 Henry VIII goes to meet Francis I of France at the Field of the Cloth of Gold in 1520. A new town of tents and pavilions has been set up to house those involved. Political discussions, however, gave way to time spent in chivalric competitions.

great horses, running geldings for racing, hacks, hunters, pack horses and carriage horses. Landowners were still expected to supply horses for the cavalry. However, in Queen Elizabeth's reign there seems to have been a certain amount of difficulty in raising these horses for the army. Landowners were reluctant and there was no effective method to ensure that they did breed suitable horses. At the time when she feared a Spanish invasion, Elizabeth had only 3,000 horsemen, although she had 30,000 men. Certainly, at the beginning of Charles I's reign, horses seem to have been considered of little value. Sir Edward Harwood obviously saw the significance of the horse in the defence of the country, however. He warned the king of the decline in the number of war horses. Probably, fewer than 2,000 could be found at that time. He said that this was because the nobility were indifferent to the raising of military horses and were more concerned with spending their money on racehorses.

The Duke of Newcastle was a great expert of the time on horses. A keen trainer and breeder of horses, he wrote the *General System of Horsemanship* and became equestrian tutor to Charles II.

of the soldier caring for, feeding and protecting his own horse — believing that each depended on the other. He saw speed and manoeuvrability as the two great essences of horse warfare. Cromwell learnt from Rupert (who fought for the Royalists) and his mistakes. Rupert used charges to scatter the enemy and then pursued them with the pistol. But having charged, his men did not keep together and pursued the enemy in total disarray, each hoping for personal gain and, as a result, there was little discipline. Cromwell insisted on small details. His horses were well-protected and held back rather than rushing out in full charge. He won his battles by maintaining an orderly cavalry formation and in 1651 defeated the Royalists at the Battle of Worcester, taking more than 10,000 prisoners.

17 Oliver Cromwell with his troops, the Roundheads, in the background.
▼

▲
16 Charles I in his armour. The painting is by Sir Anthony Van Dyck.

Cromwell's Model Army

Cromwell was the next person to concern himself with the horse and its usefulness in war. He saw the disadvantages of the slow coursers, or great horses, and the advantages of swift Arabs which he imported and incorporated into his army. Cromwell remodelled, trained and disciplined his army, which became, in effect, the first British standing army. His men were supplied with the best possible horses, carrying as little weight as possible. They were well looked after, for Cromwell founded the principle

18 Travelling by coach in 1597.

Charles II's Regiments

Charles II, following Cromwell's example, spent a lot of money importing oriental horses and liked them to match, for ceremonial parades. He also formed his own personal regiments for protection. He called them the Household Cavalry, the Life Guards, the Royal Horse Guards and the King's Dragoon Guards.

Carriages and Coaches

Travelling was now becoming easier. Horse-drawn carriages with a primitive form of suspension were in use by the 1500s. The body was suspended by leather straps fixed to vertical wooden supports at the front and back.

In the 1550s a new type of vehicle appeared in Europe, closed and larger than the open carriages and designed to carry four people inside. It was called a coach after the town of its origin, Kotze in Hungary. William Rippon built the first recorded coach in Britain in 1555 and Queen Mary had one in 1556. In 1564 Queen Elizabeth acquired a coach and in 1571 the first coach was used by her for the opening of Parliament. We also have a record of a journey she made in 1572 to Warwick, behind six big horses. At first, these coaches were owned only by the wealthy and pulled by great horses at a walking pace.

But coaches gradually improved in comfort and general design. They were ornately decorated and regarded as a luxury. Some people even saw them as an extravagance

21

and a public nuisance. Taxes were imposed on them, as a source of royal revenue, and they became more and more a symbol of status and prestige.

Road Maintenance

Roads, however, were in an appalling state and there were constant complaints about them. The General Highways Act of 1555 ordered local authorities to insist that parishioners devoted time to road repairs, but little was done and many roads remained impassable in winter. It was not until the 1660s that the Turnpike Toll System was introduced, to obtain payment from travellers for road maintenance. Tolls were levied at bars or pikes placed across the road on posts. However, these were only introduced on the major roads.

Stage Coaches

Stage coaches were introduced during the seventeenth century and were probably in use by the 1640s, and so for the first time the less well-to-do had a new means of transport. The stage coach acquired its name because it travelled from one designated point to another — in stages — on a regular scheduled journey. Journeys were long and slow, with six or eight passengers packed inside. A journey from London to Oxford took two days and to York a week. As coaches drew up at the inns, there would be fresh relays of horses waiting to relieve the tired ones.

Highwaymen

In the 1600s highwaymen were another danger, frequently attacking travellers. Soldiers who had fought in the Civil War and were now unemployed often turned to highway robbery and in 1649 General Fairfax ordered that the army should take action against highwaymen.

19 A horse-powered powder mill for grinding tan (oak bark or other material used for tanning).

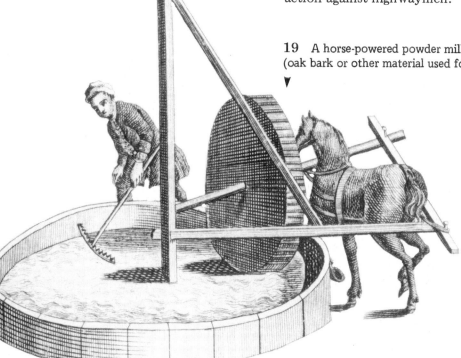

At Work on the Farms

During the 1500s and 1600s the horse continued to play a more and more important part on the farm, as methods of agriculture improved. Marshland — the Fens, in particular — was drained and fields were enclosed. An increasing amount of land was used to grow corn and also for hay. Oxen were used less as horses took their place, ploughing and harrowing, pulling horse-hoes, wagons and carts. The plough was still very simple. It had one blade to bite into the earth and turn it up and two handles, steered by a man, and it was drawn by one or two horses. The driver, besides steering the plough, guided the horses by cords, in place of reins, or by speaking to them (plough horses were trained in the dialect of their particular locality).

Horses were also being used to power machines. The horse-drawn corn mill, for example, was in use in the 1500s and 1600s. Early threshing machines were worked by either oxen or donkeys and, gradually, horses were also used, just as they began to take over from the oxen on the farms. Corn mills, butter churns, as well as threshing machines, were all worked by wheels which the horses powered by walking round and round in circles.

Horse Racing — the "Sport of Kings"

The Tudors and Stuarts were keen sportsmen. It was natural for horsemen to race against each other and during the 1500s many informal race meetings were being held. These were enlivened by betting and

20 The last race run before Charles II in 1684 at Datchet Ferry, near Windsor. The king had himself inaugurated racing here.

▼

soon became popular. During the reigns of Henry VII and Henry VIII races were held at court, in towns and among country gentry. Henry VIII kept racing horses at Greenwich and ran them in matches at Hampton Court. English kings ever since have raced horses. Chester was the first town to establish municipal racing in the early 1550s and other towns soon followed, including Doncaster, Salisbury and Richmond. There were no rules or weights. The races were run for wagers, which were often a cow or a bag of oats.

James I was keen on racing and gave it the stamp of royal approval. He imported Arabian stallions, to breed faster and lighter horses. James's favourite area for hunting was Newmarket. The court followed him there and racing followed the court. Charles I also raced there, but it was Charles II who really established racing at Newmarket as the Sport of Kings. The Rowley Mile at Newmarket was named after his favourite hack. The English were now learning the benefits of careful and selective breeding and the racecourse was the best testing ground for speed, stamina and courage of horses as a guide to selection of breeding

stock. It was not until the 1700s, though, that the thoroughbred emerged as the English Race Horse, that is, the breed used exclusively for racing.

Hunting — Deer, Hare and Fox

English sportsmen of the sixteenth and seventeenth centuries hunted deer if they were of high social status and the hare if they were not. The Tudor kings, especially Henry VIII, were keen huntsmen. In Queen Elizabeth's time the deer was still the favourite beast of the chase. Queen Elizabeth herself rode to hounds even in her seventies. It was said of her: "Every second day she is on horseback and continues the sport long". The Tudors preferred to hunt their deer in enclosed parks and kill them with arrows. Outside the parks, the majority of people depended on the hare and hunted with hare-hounds. The fox was still regarded as vermin. This was partly because it was uneatable, as Oscar Wilde later remarked in his famous lines: "The English country gentleman galloping after the fox, the unspeakable in full pursuit of the uneatable", and partly because the fox was thought of as a cunning thief and unworthy of a heroic death. So fox-hunting tended to be the sport of rural squires and yeomen and too undignified for

21 Death of the stag, 1671.

▼

nobles. It was not until the late 1600s that fox-hunting acquired a royal glamour; James II hunted foxes. In those days fox-hunting was usually a slow affair; the morning was spent in covert and there were few if any fences to be jumped and little galloping.

Drag Hunting

Drag hunting was a form of hunting whose origins can be traced to a sport promoted by the Stuarts, called "trail scenting" (hound racing). The hounds raced and the supporters rode, because it was the best way of seeing the hounds. Later, this developed into formal drag hunting, with a scent laid over prepared country.

22 Marocco, Bankes's horse, was trained to perform all sorts of tricks.

▼

Performing Horses

Finally, in those times, performing animals were a popular form of entertainment. We know that as early as the Middle Ages horses were taught to do complicated tricks. There are pictures of them rearing up, engaged in mock fights with their masters, or standing on their forelegs and beating on a small drum with their hindlegs. But the famous performing horse in Elizabethan times was Marocco. He would dance, rear and lie down at his master's command. He could also tap out with his hoof the numbers turned up on a dice. In 1600 Thomas Bankes, his owner, rode him to the top of St Paul's steeple. In Italy Marocco's abilities were regarded as black magic and Bankes and his horse were ordered to be burnt to death. Bankes, however, returned safely to England. Marocco's fate is unfortunately not known.

4
The 1700s

The Duke of Marlborough

After the Civil War the Cromwellian tradition continued in the British army. The first great cavalry leader of the century was the Duke of Marlborough (1650-1722). He insisted on discipline and never allowed his cavalry to advance faster than a trot. Like Cromwell, he believed that a man and horse must be one and that the quality of both was of the utmost importance. His cavalry was not allowed to charge and scatter in disarray over the battlefield. Marlborough's victory at Blenheim in 1704 showed the success of his training. Compared with his achievements, Europe made little progress, with the exception of Frederick the Great and Napoleon. For example, George II and his son, the Duke of Cumberland, were defeated at the Battle of Dettingen in 1743 by the French. When terrified by musket fire, both their horses bolted, and the king returned to battle without his horse.

23 The Battle of Blenheim in 1704, at which the Duke of Marlborough defeated the French and Germans. (Blenheim was a village in Germany.)
▼

Horse Regiments

▲
24 The turnpike at Tottenham Court Road in 1813.

Although the Duke of Marlborough was turning out disciplined men and horses, the average general of this time bothered little about detailed training of horse regiments, using his horsemen on the wings of his infantry battalions mainly to forage and only occasionally to charge.

In the 1700s efforts were made to raise a number of dragoon horse regiments. Dragoons, who were mounted infantrymen, were taught to fire muskets from the saddle. At first, they were light-horsed without armour and used only for light military duties, but gradually they were absorbed into the regular cavalry. And now in the eighteenth century a move began towards a light rather than a heavy cavalry, and Arabian horses were bought to improve the breeding of cavalry horses.

The dragoons were not very successful in battle because their musket range was short and muskets were difficult to carry on horseback. The cavalry attacked by trotting forward, firing, wheeling round and then retreating to reload, which hardly made use of a horse's speed and mobility. Because of this, Marlborough gave swords rather than pistols to his cavalry at the Battle of Blenheim.

Frederick the Great's Prussian Cavalry

Frederick the Great, on the other hand, took advantage of his horses' speed and manoeuvrability. He mounted his Prussian cavalry on light, agile horses, and taught his men to charge, sword in hand. He won many battles, and other leaders soon followed his example. Frederick the Great also developed the first really manoeuvrable horse artillery, with mobile cannons drawn by six horses, providing valuable support for his cavalry.

25 A packed stage coach — the passengers are going to Bury Fair in 1770.

26 Dick Turpin jumps the toll gate on his famous Black Bess. Dick Turpin was a highwayman who is said to have lived in the early 1700s and to have been hung at York for highway robbery and smuggling. His legendary ride from London to York on Black Bess is described in the poem "Rockwood" by W. H. Ainsworth.

28

Training Riders

Equitation and good horsemanship advanced in the eighteenth century. Riding schools had been started in the 1500s in Italy and one in Naples, run by Federico Grisone, was particularly famous, attracting riders from all over Europe. The English saw that horses and riders trained in Haute Ecole were more effective in battle. The Earl of Pembroke, concerned with the standard of riding in the British cavalry, wrote a book on equitation called *A Method of Breaking Horses and Teaching Soldiers to Ride*, designed for the use of the army, in which he emphasized the importance of organizing men into cavalry units. However, his attempts to improve standards did not make a great difference and the cavalry was never as great again as it had been under Cromwell or Marlborough.

Developments in Road Transport

In the early 1700s the roads were in a very poor condition. The Parish was still responsible for the upkeep of many of the roads, but still failed to do it, since there was no local or central authority. However, towards the end of the 1700s many turnpike acts were passed and gradually the turnpike toll system improved. Toll gates took the place of the old turnpikes and toll houses were built for the pikemen who collected the tolls.

Pack horses still travelled the roads, especially in winter, and carried almost anything. Sometimes as many as forty horses moved together in a long line which was known as a train.

Better roads led to better coaches. The spring was invented, and coaches were hung on steel springs which made them much more comfortable. They were more manoeuvrable, so were drawn by lighter horses which were able to travel faster on the improved roads.

27 The mail coach has stuck during a blizzard and is abandoned. Someone rides on with the mail.

In 1784 especially fast coaches began to carry the mail, which had hitherto been delivered by mounted postboys. The first mail coach under the direction of His Majesty's Post Master General ran from Bristol to London. It carried four passengers as well as mail and was drawn by a pair of horses which were changed every eight miles. The first trip was instigated by John Palmer who claimed that the mounted postboys who delivered the post were slower and much more vulnerable to attack from highwaymen than a coach carrying armed guards. Palmer's coach did deliver the post faster than the postboys and so other mail coaches began to be used. Taking passengers on the mail coaches helped to make the running costs less.

By the end of the 1700s stage and mail coaches were running regularly and kept to a time-table. Each coach had a guard, armed with a blunderbuss to use against highwaymen. His duty was to see that the coach kept time and he could be seen blowing his horn to clear the road, wake up the toll-keeper and warn hostlers waiting with fresh teams of horses. If a coach broke down, one of the leaders would be mounted and the mail carried on while the passengers were abandoned.

The coachmen who drove the mail and stage coaches became very famous. They drank a great deal to keep warm in cold weather and few lived to a great age. But in the 1700s they were almost as famous as pop stars are today.

Mounted Police

Horses were used, too, in maintaining law and order. At first, dragoons, mounted infantrymen, were used against smugglers and highwaymen, but by the late 1700s we see the beginnings of a mounted police force. The first of these were known as the Bow Street Runners who were established in 1805.

Fire Engines

It was in the 1700s that fire engines began to be pulled by horses. Before this, engines had been man-handled, but by 1730 a new bigger model had been invented with shafts for horses.

Canals

Horses were also being used for another form of transport: canals were constructed and the barges were pulled along the new waterways by single horses on the towpath. A canal horse had to be steady and docile. Speed was not important, as a fast-moving barge created waves which in time were likely to erode the banks. It was in 1759 that the Duke of Bridgewater, a coal owner, built the first major canal, an entirely artificial waterway to carry his coal from his colliery to Manchester. It was such a success that during the next fifty years other canals were built and barges now carried many goods such as wool, wheat, coal, iron and quarrystone — all moved by patient large horses walking along tow-paths specially constructed for them.

Developments on the Farms

On the farms horses continued to be used extensively. They pulled the ploughs, harrows, rollers and sowers; but these had become more efficient. The sowers or drills were set on wheels; the seed was fed into the top of the machine, and discs cut thin grooves in the earth into which the seeds ran down at regularly spaced intervals. Then the horses hoed the fields to rid them of weeds and to thin the crops.

◄ 28   An early type of fire engine, 1805. The boy is actually leading the team of horses.

On the farms at this time a new sport was invented, the Drawing Match. Teams of horses competed against one another in trials of strength, pulling wagons often loaded with sand. The wheels were sunk a little into the ground, sometimes with pieces of wood against them, to make the task even

29 The horse tows a barge past the Wedgwood Factory.

more difficult. (The heaviest load ever moved by a pair of horses was eight tons in weight in Michigan, USA, 1893.)

New Racehorses and New Races

Racing was becoming more organized now. In the early 1700s the King's Plates, which had been introduced in Britain in the reign of Charles II, were still the principal races. They were more endurance tests than races, in which horses of at least four years of age carried weights and raced over a distance of between two and four miles.

Arabs, Turks and Barbs were imported and among these were three stallions to which all modern thoroughbreds can be traced: the Byerley Turk, captured from the Turks in 1686 and later ridden by his new owner, Captain Byerley, at the Battle of Boyne; the Darley Arabian, imported into England

◄ **30** "Drilling oats".

in 1704 by Mr Darley; and the Godolphin Arab, which came from Morocco to England in 1729, sold to Edward Coke of Derbyshire. These three stallions were responsible for the greatly improved quality of the British racehorse in the later part of the 1700s.

Racing became a more and more popular sport and in 1752 the Jockey Club was formed, to regularize it. A clubhouse was built at Newmarket and, although, at first, the membership consisted of a group of the most wealthy promoters of the sport, the club gradually became a powerful institution and created rules and collected fees.

The nature of the sport was changing. As horses were bred lighter and faster, races ceased to be a test of stamina and strength, and became a test of speed. The development of the thoroughbred led to the breeding of horses for racing alone. Horses matured younger and ran faster. Also, matches — races between only two horses — were replaced by races for a number of runners. With courses becoming shorter, more races could be run in an afternoon. This meant more opportunities for betting, which became an important aspect of racing. Soon, horses under five years old could be run, as they no longer needed maturity to carry weights over long distances. The immortal Eclipse ran his first race as a five-year-old and between 1769 and 1771 ran many races of the old kind of four miles or thereabouts. But the faster, shorter races were gaining ground.

In 1776 the first of the Classics (today's most prestigious races) was held. It was named the St Leger and run at Doncaster over a distance of two miles. The race was confined to three-year-olds. This race was followed shortly afterwards by the Oaks in 1778, which was run at Epsom over one and a half miles and was for fillies. Its counterpart for colts was the Derby, also run at Epsom, in 1780. The two remaining Classic races — the 2,000 Guineas for colts and 1,000 Guineas for fillies — were run at Newmarket over one mile, in 1814 and 1819 respectively. And now, after these successful three-year-old races, it was decided that races for two-year-olds should also be run. This was bad news for horses, but allowed breeders to obtain quicker returns on their

31 The end of the chase, 1795.

investments. A two-year-old race was run at Newmarket in 1786. These young thoroughbreds, though fast, could not run over long distances, and so races of less than a mile were held — the first sprinting races.

The first official Racing Calendar was published in 1778. It listed runners, handicaps and forfeits. In 1791 The General Stud Book came into being, listing all thoroughbred brood mares and stallions with their pedigrees.

Steeplechasing

Steeplechasing also began in the 1700s, in Ireland. Hunting men, wanting to prove the courage and speed of their horses, challenged one another to races across country. The first recorded race was one held in 1752 between Blake and O'Callaghan. They raced from Buttevant Church to St Leger Church, from church steeple to church steeple, hence the name steeplechasing. At first, races were run across natural country, but in 1810 a proper course was prepared at Bedford, with specially built fences. There were only two competitors, because these first steeplechases were run as matches between two riders.

Fox-hunting

Fox-hunting, which was a faster form of the old hare- and deer-hunting, became more popular in the eighteenth century. It was found that a strong-scenting, straight-running fox gave much better sport than the hares. Because of poaching and the destruction of forests for timber, deer were becoming scarce, and so noblemen, particularly the Duke of Beaufort, turned to fox-hunting. The Enclosure Acts had changed the landscape; there were now fields enclosed by fences and hedges, which riders had to jump when in full pursuit of a fox. At first, this was done slowly — often the approach was

made at the walk, or sometimes the rider actually dismounted; but gradually the pace changed and much of fox-hunting now became a headlong gallop, with long-coated unclipped horses dying of exhaustion and riders killing themselves.

In the 1760s the famous pioneers of fox-hunting were Hugo Meynell in the Midlands, Squire Farquharson in the West and Peter Beckford in the South. Meynell, master of what became one of Britain's most well-known hunts, the Quorn, made a science of hound breeding. He bred faster and lighter hounds and other masters soon followed. So the sport increased in speed, blank days (when no foxes were found) were fewer and British hounds became famous for their speed and hunting ability.

The Circus

The circus first appeared in Britain during the reign of George III. Philip Astley, the great rider of the eighteenth century, created the first circus in 1769. He ran his shows in a London amphitheatre, which was a combination of the palatial riding schools being built in Europe and the music halls. Astley ran very popular equestrian displays. He himself used to perform standing up on a cantering horse.

32 Astley's amphitheatre in 1808.

5
The
Victorian Age

Three Wars

By the 1800s the English were finding it difficult to get men to serve in regiments of cavalry. The English cavalry in the Napoleonic Wars had little importance. Most of the battles were won for England by infantry and musketry. Wellington's cavalry formed a relatively insignificant part of his force and in around 1812 there were only 9,000 cavalrymen out of a total of 70,000 carrying arms. Wellington had a few successes with the cavalry, but nothing on the scale of Napoleon's great charges. Napoleon was the great cavalry leader of the 1800s and the French cavalry was very strong. Wellington won the Battle of Waterloo but not with his cavalry. His Union and Household Brigades charged to disaster. Their initial assault was successful, but then they got out of control and charged against the main French position. Only 20 out of 1200 men of the Union Brigade reached the French lines. After the

33   The Battle of Waterloo in 1815, at which the Duke of Wellington defeated Napoleon.

war Wellington damned the British cavalry, considering them far inferior to that of the French and admitting that they could gallop but that they could not preserve their order. They were also considered careless horse masters, the horses being covered in saddle sores and girth galls.

For the rest of the century there was a decline in the use of the cavalry, as fire power became the dominant feature on the battlefield. At Crimea, one of the major wars of that period (the French and English had declared war on Russia), the cavalry did not feature. First, at the Battle of Balaclava in 1854, the British Heavy Brigade were successful. But the saddest and most famous incident of the Crimean War was The Charge of the Light Brigade, one of the most tragic events in history. The Light Brigade was ordered to attack a Russian infantry formation, but the order was vague and misunderstood and they moved against the enemy artillery. A total of 673 riders set out and only 195 returned. The event has been immortalized by Lord Tennyson's poem which ends movingly:

Storm'd at with shot and shell
While horse and hero fell,
They that had fought so well
Came thro' the jaws of Death
Back from the Mouth of Hell
All that was left of them,
Left of six hundred.

When can their glory fade?
O the wild charge they made!
All the world wonder'd.
Honour the charge they made!
Honour the Light Brigade,
Noble six hundred!

After the Crimean War, as gunfire became more devastating, horses were used less in the front line and there were few cavalry charges. However, horses were still employed in great numbers by various countries in war.

▲
34 The British cavalry drive back a Boer outpost. The Boers are wearing cowboy hats and carrying rifles.

In the Boer War, fought between the British and the South African Boer farmers from 1899-1902, horses were used by the two sides in different ways. The Boers used guerilla tactics, fighting on small sturdy ponies. These ponies, accustomed to the country and climate, could cover long distances with little effort and food. The British, used to orderly battles, were confused at first and there were many casualties, but, gradually, after they had imported thousands of horses from different parts of the world, the tide turned for them and they won the war. Over 400,000 horses, mules and donkeys perished during the Boer War, and at Kimberley many horses were eaten, there being no other food.

The Golden Age of Coaching

By 1815 roads were vastly improved. John MacAdam and Thomas Telford invented a new road surface where small stones were laid to a depth of six inches, used as a road foundation. This meant that coaches (stage and mail) could travel more easily and faster, with lighter horses. The average speed was now 10 mph and the number of coaches increased all over Britain. So the 1800s became the Golden Age of Coaching. Mail and stage coaches ran regularly and competed

35

with each other, and speed became the vital factor, both in the delivery of mail and in encouraging passengers to choose the mail rather than the stage coach for travel.

The mail coaches were at an advantage, for they had the right of way, were untaxed and paid no tolls. By 1835 there were about 700 mail coaches running, each drawn by four horses which were changed every fifteen miles. At this time there were also some 3,000 stage coaches in regular service, and stage coaches could carry more passengers, with up to twelve on top and usually eight seated at the back. The mail coaches were painted in Royal colours — black, with scarlet wheels, and maroon panels on which the monarch's initials were inscribed. Stage coaches were painted in bright colours, with names of their stopping places in gold, and sometimes they had names such as the Tally-Ho or Red Rover.

In 1832 the first hackney cabriolets appeared, which were licensed two-wheeled vehicles for hire. These competed with the hackney carriages which had increased in number during the 1700s. Hackneys were

35 George Shillibeer's omnibus. These omnibuses catered especially for passengers making short journeys.

▼

bred as draft horses and were good trotters. Also in the 1830s two-wheeled hansom cabs were introduced and four-wheeled Clarence cabs, which survived until the end of the 1800s. All these cabs were used in the towns. Wagonettes were popular in the 1800s for transport in the country, as well as open vehicles drawn by pairs or singles. They could carry a party of people and were often used for outings. In the 1840s the four-wheeled cab or growler started to replace the hackney cabs.

Driving was becoming an increasing pastime and pleasure. The wealthy travelled in their own private carriages. From the 1780s privately owned and driven four-wheeled vehicles were known as phaetons. One type, the crane-necked phaeton, was called the high flyer — a nickname — which was also given to the daring men, and sometimes women, who drove them.

For long-distance travelling, gentry who did not own their own carriages but did not wish to use the stage or mail coaches could travel post — which meant hiring post-chaises and horses from stage to stage. These post-chaises were known as yellow bounders (they were often gentlemen's discarded private travelling chariots painted yellow). They seated two passengers and were driven

36 Skinny-looking horses (just two are needed!) pulling a tram.

37 The Mountjoy Brewery dray and its prize-winning horse in 1893.

38 The daily milk float about 1910. Note the early form of sweat rug!

postillion by the postboys. Relays of horses were available at the posting houses (inns) about every ten miles along the route. Horses travelled at the gallop. The posting business was the most important part of the innkeeper's trade (so much so that some inns would refuse to take in travellers if they were not in need of horses).

In 1829 a Mr Shillibeer ran the first public omnibus and it is believed to have gone from the Haymarket to Epsom on Derby Day. In that year, too, the first regular omnibus ran, on the Paddington road. The omnibuses were spacious, with room for twenty-two passengers inside and more outside, and they were drawn by two or three horses abreast. The service was often luxurious, with coachmen dressed in velvet suits and even a small library inside to help passengers relieve the boredom of travel.

By the 1840s the Golden Age of Coaching was virtually over, for the railways were providing a faster way of travelling and the steam engine was developed and replaced the horses which had pulled the wagons along the early railways. Mail and stage coaches gradually became less in number. Horse-drawn wheeled transport remained, however, both as a necessity and as a diversion during the Victorian Age.

The original trams, first seen in the 1870s, were horse-drawn, where the country was flat. The work was exhausting, for the trams were heavy, carrying more passengers than the omnibuses. Tram horses had short lives, because the constant starting and stopping put an immense strain on their legs.

The Tradesman's Horse

At this time, business would have ground to a halt without horses; they were to be seen everywhere: carrying goods, collecting rubbish, hauling coal, drawing brewers' drays laden with barrels of beer. Heavy horses were used for most of these tasks. Tradesmen used horses called "vanners" to deliver

39 Bathing machines in Budlington Bay, Yorkshire, in 1813.

their goods. These were not breeds but types — small, light-legged cart horses which worked at a brisk trot, delivering milk, vegetables, bread and fish. The butchers had the fastest trotters, the forebears of the modern hackney, and they were the carriers, too, which carried passengers and goods from the countryside to the town. Horses had one rather extraordinary task which was to pull bathing machines (huts on wheels) down the beach to the edge of the sea, from which ladies would emerge in bathing costumes. It was not thought decent to be seen wandering around in one's swimwear!

Horse-Power

As farming methods improved, horses became more essential to the farmer. Oxen could no longer match a horse's speed and efficiency. Many new machines invented in the 1800s, such as reaping and mowing

◄ **40** Horses hauling timber from a wood being cleared in Kent.

machines and tedders for spreading hay, needed horse-power.

Horses were used extensively for hauling timber and here great strength was needed, as horses had to haul tree trunks on to timber drays as well as pull the laden carts to their destination. Teams of six or more horses were harnessed to the pole wagons. Horses were particularly practical for the job and their hoofs, in fact, did less damage to young trees than the machinery of today.

Stronger horses were slowly developing. Shire horses had been carefully bred before the formation of the breed society in 1878 and their first stud book. In 1878 the Clydesdale's stud book was started, but like the Shires, pedigree Clydesdales were being bred before the formation of their breed society in 1877. Suffolk Punches are first mentioned at the end of the 1700s and, carrying almost no feather on their legs, were ideal for ploughing in heavy soil, such as is found in East Anglia. Percherons were imported from France, but not until 1900.

At this time, horses were also used for moving machinery. The portable steam engines, invented in the 1800s, could not move under their own steam and so horses transported them from mills to threshing machines. So horse-power came into being, measured by the number of horses needed to move a particular engine, which could be four, six, eight or ten.

Pit Ponies

In the 1840s the first pit ponies were used in the coal mines; for in 1842 the Mines Act forbade the employment of boys and girls in the mines to pull the coal tubs. Before this time there were no mechanical hoists capable of carrying ponies down the shafts. So horses had been used only at the pit-heads to cart the coal away. Now, ponies could pull coal tubs underground, along the railway tracks.

Modern Flat Racing

By Victorian times the thoroughbred was world-famous and being exported to many different countries as foundation stock. The squires were largely responsible for modern racing and for the creation of the thoroughbred. With the founding of the Jockey Club in 1752, the word "jockey" had been born and soon professional trainers and bookmakers followed. By the middle of the 1800s today's format of racing had been established. Long-distance races disappeared and ones for two-year-olds became common. These were between five and seven furlongs in length (a furlong being 220 yards). There were also one-to-one and three-quarter-mile races, and races over one and three quarter miles for the older horses, with more staying power. The flat racing season extended from March to November.

The Grand National

During the early 1800s steeplechases became organized races over marked courses. By the 1830s the sport had become much more popular and in 1839 the first Grand National was held at Aintree near Liverpool. The race was four miles across country and seventeen competitors entered, including a certain Captain Becher. The first fence was post and rails, with a brook on the landing side, and here Captain Becher fell into the brook, horse and all. Since that day, this fence, though no longer the first, has been called Becher's Brook. A horse called Lottery won the first race and one horse died.

In 1866 the Grand National Hunt Steeplechase Committee was set up and this later became known as the National Hunt Committee. It now controls the sport and has powers analogous to those of the Jockey Club in flat racing. So, gradually, steeplechasing ceased to be merely a race for wagers or solely a schooling ground for hunters and became an organized sport.

Hunts started to run their own races which were called point-to-points and were largely local meetings. They were amateur events for inexperienced jockeys and for keen hunting men. These first point-to-points like the early steeplechases, were run from one vantage point to another across country. But, gradually, they became more organized and in 1885 were recognized by the National Hunt Committee.

The Golden Age of Fox-Hunting

But steeplechasing in the 1800s still took second place to fox-hunting in the eyes of the country squires, such as Squire Osbaldeston, who considered steeplechasing nothing less than "rough" riding. By this time a combination of faster, more agile and enduring horses, hounds with drive as well as speed and a country with better drainage, enclosed by fields and hedges meant that ditches and post and rail fences could be ridden over at a gallop. Horses and riders died in pursuit of hounds and Surtees, a famous sporting author, called hunting "the image of war without its guilt and only 25% of its danger".

41 "The enraged Vicar", by Rowlandson, 1808. The hunt goes on, regardless of where the fox runs.

It was really the Golden Age of fox-hunting between 1820 and 1890, before barbed wire and motor cars changed the landscape. MacAdam's new metalled roads helped followers to travel long distances to hunts. And although the railways cut parts of the countryside in half, the trains were soon transporting horses long distances to meets, and a special train was run to Leicestershire solely for this purpose; for the best hunting was to be found in Leicestershire and Rut-

42 The opening match of the polo club at Hurlingham in 1874.

land. Escaping the Corn Laws, these counties had large expanses of grass and good scenting conditions.

In 1881 the Master of Foxhounds Association was formed, laying down certain rules and standards which still exist today.

43   An early policeman of the Stratford-upon-Avon Division, seen here with his groom, 1912.

Polo

Polo also arrived in England in the 1800s. We have references to show that it was played in the time of Alexander the Great; but its first players were thought to have been Persians around 600 BC. The game then spread East to the Chinese and Mongolians and from there to India. In the 1850s British planters in India brought the game to England, and in 1869 the tenth Hussars started playing the game officially. At first, the soldiers used their chargers for the game, but soon they changed to smaller animals which were to be called polo ponies. Hurlingham became the headquarters of polo and in 1875 the Hurlingham Association was formed and drew up rules.

Victorian Show Jumping

Show jumping also originated in the late 1800s. In those days it was an expansion of other outdoor equestrian activities in which jumping took place, such as point-to-points, steeplechases and hunting. The course was made up of natural jumps in the arena — banks, walls, water jumps and wooden fences. These competitions were used primarily to assess the ability of hunters, and points were given for style. If a fence was knocked, however gently, a fault was given.

The Value of Horses

Throughout the Victorian Age horses were used in the police forces for patrolling the streets and parks, to keep them safe. They

44   The Annual Horse Fair at Horncastle, Lincoln-
shire, in 1864.

were still an essential part of the nation; thousands were stabled in town, many were turned out for yearly holidays in the country. But others hardly saw a blade of grass the whole year round. Most of them were old horses by the time they were fifteen, worn-out by years of work; but some were much loved and appreciated by their owners, who would have a hoof turned into a paper-weight after a favourite horse died.

Horses in the Victorian Age were being exploited to the full in war, industry, the transport system and for sport. Had horses gone on strike, the whole economy would have come to a halt! Horse fairs were common annual events to which professional and amateur horsedealers and breeders, owners of coaches and omnibuses, job-masters, gentlemen sportsmen and cavalry mount agents all came en masse. At these fairs a marvellous collection of different types of horses for different uses could be seen: harness horses and hunters made high prices (good jumpers making anything up to £200). Strong, thick-set, active horses suitable for town vans or carriers' light carts brought up to £50. Well-built horses for artillery and other military work and cart horses also brought up to £50. Saddle horses, however, made more — £90 to £140.

6
The 1900s—
Two World Wars

On the Battlefield

The horse still played a useful part in warfare when the First World War broke out. There were more than a million cavalry poised for action. Many of these were sent to France and were used on the Western Front. The plan was to use the cavalry to gallop through a breach to be made in the enemy's line by the infantry, and to turn the enemy's defeat into a rout. It is said that they were to gallop through the "g" (gap). For two years the cavalry was kept ready at great expense, but no breakthrough came. When, on occasion, the cavalry did act, it was only to suffer great losses. The infantry were often led by mounted officers whose horses had little chance of survival.

In 1917, during the Battle of Arras, tanks captured Monchy-Le-Preux and the cavalry moved up after them only to meet hails of bullets. Nothing was gained and there were many casualties. Again, at the Battle of Amiens in 1918, three cavalry divisions were sent forward to wipe out units already destroyed by tanks, but they got in each other's way and the attack was a

45   Battle of the Canal du Nord in September 1918. The horses are pulling guns. Gun teams were reduced from six to four horses, so that the extra horses could be supplied to the Americans.

▼

46 These Surrey yeomanry are retreating to the Hindenburg line in 1917.

disaster. Tanks were certainly proving to be a more satisfactory means of going into battle. Overall, however, with trenches, barbed wire and the power of the machine guns, it was clear that the cavalries could not be used extensively.

But large numbers of horses were still needed for draught work. Artillery was the main weapon of attack and, with guns becoming bigger and heavier, it was necessary to have teams of horses to move them. Horses were also used to pull field ambulances, and pack horses carried ammunition. The conditions everywhere on the battleground were terrible, and horses had to wade through fields of mud and large pools, dug by explosives, deep enough to drown in. It was recorded by Sir Frederick Hobday, a veterinary surgeon working in the middle of the war years, that in one year over 120,000 horses were treated for wounds and diseases.

The First World War had shown that, with new developments in army tactics and a greater sophistication of weapons, the horse was really a futile piece of equipment to use against the enemy. Cavalry regiments, however, were only reduced from 28 to 20. Many army men still believed that the age of

◄ 47 The Battle of Pilckem Ridge, near Ypres. Shell-carrying pack mules are struggling through the mud. The year is 1917.

the horsed warrior was not passed. In 1926, for example, Haig wrote:

I believe that the value of and opportunities for the horse in future are likely to be as great as ever . . . aeroplanes and tanks are only accessories to the man and the horse . . .

Debates about the importance of the cavalry continued in the thirties. Politicians concerned with military affairs knew that mechanization must replace the horse, but the change was not completed by 1939. During the Second World War horses were still used, but only where land proved impassable for the tanks.

After 1945 cavalry horses were still used in various parts of the world — in Malaya, where fighting took place in the jungle, horses were extremely useful, especially pack horses. In Russia, cavalries were maintained and used where conditions remained terrible. Poland still had a superb cavalry which charged the German tanks with im-

mense bravery, only to be totally destroyed. British horses were used against guerillas, mainly in Kenya during the Mau Mau emergency, and there the last British cavalry operation took place in 1953, when a detachment of the North Frontier Tribal Police came across a guerilla camp and attacked them successfully.

For thousands of years the horse had proved to be man's speed, strength and saviour in war. Now, at last, machines had taken over. However, the traditions of the famous horse brigades remain in the ceremonial regiments which perform for the public, regularly reviving the heritage which made Britain great.

Remaining Horse Transport

By the beginning of the twentieth century the coaching industry, which had waned

45

◄ 49 A Phaeton being driven in 1912 by Midge and Billy.

was a double-decker with rows of forward-facing seats.

After the First World War the motor car began to replace horse transport, but many still preferred to be driven by their coachmen in private carriages such as Landaus, Barouches and Broughams. Others enjoyed driving themselves in dog carts and phaetons, often drawn by ponies. Gigs were popular and, in particular, Stanhope gigs. The Governess cart was introduced about 1900, specially designed for children and often driven by the nursery governess.

Coaching as a sport, however, was developing rapidly and various coaching and driving clubs were formed. So, throughout this period of change, revolutionizing the transport system, the desire to drive remained. Between the wars a few stage

ever since the arrival of the railways, had been partially revived. Sportsmen had seen to it that stage coaches were put back on their original roads and so, during the reign of Edward VII (1901-1910), coaches seem to have been popular. However, with the outbreak of the First World War, both horses and men were conscripted and coaching routes were once again hardly used.

During the early 1900s horses were still being used in industry, transporting goods along railway lines and for delivery services. In towns, omnibuses, trams and hansom cabs were still running. The garden seat omnibus was the later form of omnibus; it

50 The last horse-drawn mail van leaving the post office, Penzance.
▼

▲
51 Gypsies and their pair of either skewbalds or piebalds being overtaken by a juggernaut – which proves that they can still be seen on the roads today.

coaches were run yet again to their original destinations, such as Oxford and Brighton.

With the outbreak of the Second World War, the sport of coaching ended, but afterwards, when petrol restrictions came into force, once again people were using carriages for practical purposes. Driving as a sport was also taken up once more and post-war shows held coaching classes.

Other wheeled vehicles still on the roads were the wagons of the gypsies. Many gypsies could still be seen travelling through Britain, with their wagons and horses, in the 1930s. The horses had to be strong, quiet and docile. Typically, they were piebald or skewbald, the coloured horse being particularly favoured by the travelling gypsies.

particularly efficient in the work of drilling and sowing. It was important that rows of corn should be accurate and today's evidence of irregular tractor drilling goes to show how much more exact cart horses could be!

During the mid-twenties the tractor started to be used on farms and, as more and more farmers adopted this new form of power, the working horse was threatened. However, the change-over was slow and up until the outbreak of the Second World War it was still common to see the horse ploughing, cultivating, sowing and reaping.

The Tractor Takes Over

During the early 1900s horses were the mainstay on the farm and in 1930 farmers in England and Wales still had over 800,000 horses working on their farms. Horses were

Down the Mines

Ponies were still important in industry, especially in mining. The ponies lived down the mines. They were stabled underground, and received fresh air from the surface.

47

AGRICULTURAL EDUCATION.

Farmer (to lad put to ploughing for the first time.) "What on earth be at, messin' about all over the place like this?"
Farm Lad. "Wull, you told I to look at summat an' go straight to it, an' I bin tryin' to foller thic ther cow till I be tired, an' now I be waiting for 'er to lie down!"

52 An agricultural education, *Punch*, 1909.

The stables were electrically lit, and had concrete or brick floors. A pony continued to work as long as he was fit and the average working life was ten to fifteen years. They worked a six and a half hour day. Strict regulations governed the use of pit ponies: their hours of work, maximum loads and working conditions. The ponies did not go blind as is sometimes thought and were examined regularly by vets and at least once a year by a horse inspector.

In the early 1900s there were 70,000 ponies in the mines. But, as the mines were more mechanized, the number dropped. By the 1950s there were only about 17,000. The ponies were gradually replaced by rope haulage and conveyors driven by electric engines or by locomotives. In some places, though, machinery could not be installed and the pony continued to be used. Most ponies were used in Northumberland and Durham coalfields. Here the seams of coal were thin and small Welsh ponies and Shetlands had to be used. In Yorkshire and the Midlands seams were bigger and ponies up to 14 hh could be employed, whilst in South Wales even bigger seams meant that colliery horses up to 15 hh, often crosses between Cobs and Shires, could be used.

53 A miner with his pit pony in South Wales. ➤

Sports continued to develop during the twentieth century, although they were somewhat hampered during the world wars.

Until the First World War the Grand National was the all-important steeplechasing event of the year, but by 1920 the sport became more widely spread and steeplechasing was taking place on many courses all over Britain. However, the Grand National was a handicap race, and there were no races to discover the best horses at even weights. So, in 1924 the Cheltenham Gold Cup, a race of three and a quarter miles, was instituted for this purpose. By the 1930s the famous steeplechaser Golden Miller had won the Cheltenham Gold Cup five times and the Grand National once.

Flat racing continued to be popular, and some race meetings were held even throughout the wars. The Triple Crown, which is awarded to a horse who wins the 2,000 Guineas, the Derby and the St Leger, was won by Gainsborough in 1918. Gainsborough's famous son was Hyperion. He was a small horse, just 15.2½ hands high, but won both the Derby and the St Leger in the 1930s.

At the close of the nineteenth century roads, railways and enclosures were influencing hunting. Guns improved and pheasant shooting became more popular. The pheasant versus fox-hunting controversy began.

Hunting was an expensive sport and by the end of the century few private packs remained. Nearly all were subscription packs which meant that sportsmen had to pay subscriptions to help finance them. Despite all this, fields (i.e. people out hunting) became larger and women began to appear in increasing numbers, riding side-saddle. Farmers also supported hunting, often riding to hounds themselves.

Hunting was naturally curtailed during the Great War. Many horses as well as the youth of Great Britain were lost. Then cars replaced horses and grooms became mechanics. Many sportsmen thought that hunting could never be revived. But it did survive. The Prince of Wales hunted regularly and, with a wider distribution of wealth, a new breed of people were ready to ride to hounds.

54   A double spill at the Old Berks point-to-point, 1936.
▼

After the Second World War fox-hunting became more of a controversial subject. There were those opposed to hunting because they thought the killing and triumph in the death of the fox cruel and unnecessary. Others thought that it was an effective and humane method of keeping the fox population down, regarding shooting, gassing and trapping and poisoning as far crueller means of death. To some extent, hunts did stop their displays of triumph in killing their fox — no longer initiating children into hunting by smearing them with the blood of the fox, for example and no longer mounting the mask, brushes and pads of the fox.

55   An early cross country event. The rider wears ▶ no hat and the horse is without a noseband.

56   The Duke of Beaufort leads the hunt. The Badminton Estate is seen in the background.
▼

The Development of Show Jumping

Show jumping was a sport still very much in its beginnings. Before 1914 show jumps had consisted of natural fences such as banks, walls and water jumps. Slats were placed on top of all the jumps so that, if they were knocked off, points were deducted. Now, new jumps began to develop, such as triples, parallels and oxers (brush fences with rails set out on one side). Combinations such as doubles and trebles (three jumps one after the other) were also used. Course builders began to vary the distances separating fences, as well as their shapes. Different types of competition developed. There were jump-offs without being against the clock, but the against-the-clock jump-offs were more exciting and called for speed and handiness. There were also pure speed competitions, such as Take Your Own Line (riders choose their own way around a course of jumps). In a normal jumping competition, though, style was still very important and marks were given for it.

The first Royal International Horse Show was held at Olympia as early as 1907 and revived after the First World War in 1920. After the Second World War it was transferred to the White City. In 1921 the "Fédération Equestre Internationale" was founded. The FEI was founded mainly by France and Sweden, because it was thought that rules for equestrian events in the Olympic Games should be standardized. Gradually, more and more countries became affiliated to the FEI and Britain joined in 1925. In Britain in 1923 the British Show Jumping Association was formed to draw up rules and set standards. The BSJA thus improved things, varying what had been very monotonous courses and improving judging standards.

After the Second World War Michael Ansell, though blind, did much for show jumping. Rules were altered, riders being no longer allowed to take as long as they wanted to complete a course. Previously they had walked between jumps if they wished and circled before fences (to make sure that their horses were on the right stride). The slats on jumps had made accuracy all-important. There was even a distinction between hitting a fence with the fore and hindlegs. Gradually, these rules were abolished.

The great show jumpers riding after the war were people like Harry Llewellyn and his horse Foxhunter and Pat Smythe with Tosca.

Horse Trials

Horse trials were originally invented as a test for the officer's charger and were known as "the military". The soldiers were naturally keen to do well if there was a championship as a reward. Later, civilians also took part and the sport became known as eventing. There were three-day events, in which the whole competition took that length of time, or one-day events. Nowadays horse trials provide the all-round test for horse and rider and consist of three parts — dressage, cross country with steeplechase and track phase, and show jumping.

A three-day event was first included in the Olympic Games in 1912, but there were

57 Horses of all different shapes and sizes fill the ring at Bertram Mills Circus.

▼

no national competitions in Britain until after the 1948 Olympic Games at Aldershot and Wembley. The idea of a three-day event to be held annually in Britain was conceived by the Duke of Beaufort while he watched the Olympic three-day event of 1948. The British Horse Society agreed to support the idea of a three-day event at Beaufort's Badminton estate in Gloucestershire and so in April 1949 the first event was held, with twenty-two riders taking part. After Badminton, more three-day events were established, although one-day events (which had no steeplechase and track phase) were not being held until the fifties.

Gymkhanas

In the early 1900s small horse shows were held, incorporating other events which were called gymkhanas. Gymkhana is an Anglo-Indian word which first appeared in 1861 and meant a place for an athletic display. To the Indians during British rule, it just meant pony races with betting. Early gymkhanas in Britain were still races on ponies, but of different types, such as bending, sack and apple and bucket races. People still used to bet on the competitors and, at first, adults only took part, but by the 1930s more and more gymkhanas were run for children. The Handy Hunter class was also a popular event. This was timed and often included jumping a few special fences, opening a gate and leading your pony over a jump.

The Pony Club

Children riding in these gymkhanas were often members of the newly founded Pony Club. This was begun in 1929, to encourage young people to ride and enjoy the sport connected with horses and ponies, and to teach children to ride as well as look after their ponies. It provided instruction and lessons in stable management, as well as entertainment. In 1930, just a year later, the Pony Club had 700 members and in 1931 the membership was 4,442, but the real boom came after the war in the late 1940s, when membership was over 17,000. Nowadays membership has risen to over 50,000.

Horses in the Circus

Lastly, horses continued to provide entertainment for the public. Circuses had become very popular, and horses were a major attraction at these shows. The riders trained the horses to perform complicated manoeuvres. Lipizzaners, Arabs and Andalusians were the main breeds used and there were three different types of circus horses. The Liberty horses were and still are usually Anglo-Arabs or pure-bred Arabs, and ponies such as Shetlands were also used. The Liberty horses are trained to do acts by themselves and come when called by their trainers. They perform often in pairs and so must match in colour. The Rosinbacks (or Resinbacks) is the name given by the circus to bareback riding horses. The name originates from the fact that resin is rubbed on the horse's back and quarters to prevent the performer from slipping. The riders vault, jump or stand on the horses' backs. Only horses of quiet temperaments can be used and they must have very steady canters. Lastly, there are the high school horses. These perform various high school acts such as the piaffe, which is a cadenced high trot done on the spot, the capriole, in which the horse makes a half rear and jumps forward and up in the air, kicking the hindlegs out, and the levade, in which the horse raises its forefeet and draws them in, all the weight being supported by the hindlegs. The horses perform these acts to music and some even dance, stepping in time to a waltz or tango. The Liberty and high school acts are performed at Mary Chipperfield's Circus.

54

7
Horses Today

Today, horses are used extensively by people of all ages for sport and leisure. In this modern day the horse is no longer really necessary for practical purposes. There are a few exceptions; police horses, for example, are practical for use in cities. Royal and ceremonial horses continue to be used and remind us of our traditions. Then, in some places, heavy horses are making a comeback on the farms and being used to pull brewery drays and other vehicles. However, the majority of horses in Britain are used to give pleasure, either in competitions or by being ridden at leisure.

58 A sack race at a small gymkhana.
▼

59　A small competitor jumps a large fence!

Horse Shows

Horse shows are held all over Britain between April and October, giving enjoyment to both riders and spectators and incorporating many different types of competition. The shows help to stimulate trade, because here the breeders and producers of horses can show their horses to the public and hope to sell them.

There are small local shows which cater for children living in the area and whose main attraction is often the gymkhana events. There are bigger regional shows, where riders may qualify with their horses for other competitions, and then there are important international shows, such as the Horse of the Year Show, in which top riders of Britain and those from abroad compete.

The small shows typically have a couple of arenas. In one, the jumping takes place. There are classes for different age groups and sizes of horses. For example, the first class is often for ponies of 12.2 hands high and under, ridden by children of 12 years of age and under. There may well be a novice class for riders who have not won prizes on their ponies before. In the other arena, various showing classes may be taking place, such as Best Family Pony or Best Working Pony. Then there are the gymkhana classes, typically for 12s and under, and open classes. Races may well include bending, musical poles, walk, trot and canter, mug, potato and sack races. There are many other more complicated races, such as the Gretna Green race in which pairs of riders have to hold a rope between them and jump a cavaletti

(low poles resting on X's at either end).

Larger shows incorporate more competitors and use more arenas. The show classes are much grander. A show class is held to select the best specimen of a breed or type. Show classes play an important role in improving breeds, as the winners set examples of the best sort of animals for a particular purpose. There are two kinds: ridden classes and in-hand classes. In-hand classes include classes for stallions, brood mares and young stock. Ridden classes may be for hunters, hacks, cobs or ponies. Then again, hunter classes are divided into heavy, middle and light for show hunters and working hunters. The difference is that show hunters are judged on their action at walk, trot, canter and gallop, their conformation and their behaviour; working hunters have, in addition, to jump a course of rustic fences. Pony show classes are divided into those for

14.2 hh and under, 13.2 hh and under, 12.2 hh and under, and leading rein classes for small ponies ridden by small children. Turn-out of the ponies and riders is taken into account by the judges in some classes, as well as conformation and behaviour. Hunters are expected to be ridden in double bridles.

The British Show Pony Society was founded in 1949, by those who wanted better rules for show classes. They wanted to prevent cheating, as often parents would enter their over-aged children, or ponies above the height limit. The important event for the best show ponies each year is the Ponies of Britain Show at Peterborough.

The international shows continue to attract many foreigners every year. Important annual shows are the Royal Windsor Show, the Royal International Horse Show and the Horse of the Year Show, both held at Wembley, and the Hickstead Show.

The Royal International Horse Show holds showing classes for all types. Riders and their horses must have qualified for the classes at previous shows and compete here for the championships. International show jumping attracts many spectators throughout the week. The most famous show jumping classes are the Queen Elizabeth II Cup for women and the King George V Gold Cup for men.

The Horse of the Year Show holds many championships. There are competitions for the police horse of the year, junior show jumper of the year, hack and show hunter of the year. The finals of the Pony Club mounted games are held here, in which teams compete for the Prince Philip Cup.

Show jumping is often the main feature at these big shows. Gone are the days of a course of six jumps with no time limits. Course building has become an art in itself. Courses have become big, complicated and more diverse than before, with difficult combinations of jumps such as parallel bars followed closely by uprights.

Horse Trials Today

Besides show jumping, horse trials have become an integrated part of the equestrian scene. They are now a tremendous test of a horse's skill, fitness and stamina, as well as its ability to cross country, negotiating difficult obstacles at speed. It must also possess the training, calmness and fluency of a dressage horse. Finally, it must be capable of performing a show jumping course. All

61 The Harewood three-day event. The rider has to jump in and cross this small lake.

▼

this is a far cry from the early days of eventing.

Horse trials are held all over Britain. Badminton is still Britain's most famous three-day event. The Burghley horse trials are also an important event, held in September.

Driving

Driving horses for practical purposes became less important with the advent of the motor car, but after the Second World War driving started to develop as a sport. Since the 1950s more and more people have discovered the pleasure of driving horse-drawn vehicles. The Queen's coronation in 1953 inspired people with the desire to drive, on account of the procession, which was mostly horse-drawn. In 1956 the British Driving Society was formed, to help people interested in driving.

Three different types of driving have developed for those wishing to practise competitively. Coaching classes are included in most big horse shows. Teams of horses are required to pull historical coaches and are judged on turn-out and the fitness of the horses, sometimes after completing a marathon drive before appearing in the ring. Coaching is an expensive form of driving as the old coaches have to be maintained, but they are a great attraction at major shows, as symbols of a bygone era.

Private driving competitions are usually included at major shows. These are showing classes in which singles or pairs are driven round the arena and judged on their paces and behaviour as well as general turn-out. Private driving is a popular competition, as all that is required is a pretty pony and carriage, both immaculately clean and smart.

The most exciting recently developed competitions are the "combined driving" ones. The rules for these were drawn up in 1969 and the first international competition was held in 1970 at the Royal Windsor Horse Show. Combined driving is a three-day event on wheels, in which horses pull their carriages through dressage tests, across country and around an obstacle course in an arena. In the dressage section points are also given for presentation, with the cleanliness of carrige, horse and harness being taken into account, plus the horse's condition. For the dressage the horses have to collect and extend their trot and walk and rein back. The cross country phase — marathon — is exciting, as about 20 miles have to be covered at speed, through obstacles, into water and between trees. For the last phase on the third day competitors must complete a course driving through obstacles, pairs of cones, without hitting them. The Duke of Edinburgh helped in promoting this sport and is president of the FEI. He also became patron of the British Driving Society in 1973, and is himself a leading combined driving competitor. Coaching marathons are also held at separate events in large private parks such as Windsor Great Park or Eaton Hall Park.

Holidays on Horseback

Pony trekking holidays and riding holidays have become increasingly popular in recent years. Both give a great deal of enjoyment to people without horses or ponies of their own. Pony trekking has introduced many to the joys of riding and caters for beginners especially. It provides an opportunity for people to enjoy the beauties of the countryside on horseback, at a gentle pace. Pony trekking centres provide holidays of varying lengths from a weekend to a week, or even longer. Rides usually begin and end at the trekking centre each day, but there are also trail rides where nights are spent en route. Popular trekking centres have been established on Dartmoor and Exmoor and in the New Forest and the Lake District.

Riding holidays are sometimes more specialized. They usually concentrate on furthering the knowledge and ability of the rider and offer instruction in particular aspects of horsemanship such as dressage or show jumping, or even riding side-saddle. Sometimes the week ends with a horse show.

Long-Distance Riding

Long-distance riding is practised competitively. The Golden Horse-shoe ride is held every year over the Exmoor National Park and 75 miles must be covered. This is not a race, but standards are set and horses competing must be extremely fit.

Hunting Today

Today hunting is certainly an expensive sport. But despite many factors of the modern-day world which make hunting more difficult, it is as popular as ever, many riders turning out up to four days a week, others following the hunts either by car, bicycle or on foot. Land which was once 80% pasture is now often 80% ploughed land; the expansion of industry and suburbia have reduced the huntable areas; motorways and railways prove impassable barriers; use of wire has increased; intensive manuring obliterates the scent: all these factors hinder the chase. However, there are over 300 packs of hounds hunting all over Britain. The five Shire packs, the Quorn, Pytchley, Fernie, Belvoir and Cottesmore, are still the most famous.

Drag hunting packs still exist in country where motorways and wire prevent successful fox-hunting. A line of scent is prepared of anything from 7 to 15 miles and riders then follow the hounds, jumping the specially organized fences en route. As it is easier to pick up the scent of a drag, fewer hounds are needed, often only 5 to 15 couples (large fox-hunts may take out as many as 50 couples). Blood hounds hunting volun-teered human quarry is becoming an increasingly popular sport.

The Growth of Polo

After the Second World War little polo was played. Many administrators and players had been killed. Also, some famous British polo grounds were lost and ponies were scarce. The sport became very popular in Argentina. During the fifties the sport was revived in Britain. Lord Cowdray organized a club and polo grounds. In the early days of polo there had been a height limit of 14.2 hh, but later this was abolished and bigger animals are now used. Thoroughbreds or part-thoroughbreds are often used and crossed with Criollos, Argentinian horses, to produce polo ponies and the game has become much faster. (The horses are still called polo ponies even though they are often over 15 hh.) Prince Charles began playing polo at 17 and is one of Britain's top polo players. Argentina is the number one polo-playing country and today's polo-playing centres are the USA and Argentina. In the sixties the Pony Club started to play polo and hold an annual polo tournament. Some of Britain's top players started by playing in the Pony Club tournaments.

Royal Horses

Today, horses are used in royal ceremonies just as they were hundreds of years ago. Kings and queens have always regarded horses as an essential part of regalia. The Queen's carriage horses are kept at the Royal Mews at Buckingham Palace and also at Windsor Castle and Hampton Court.

The Windsor Greys, the famous carriage horses, were once stalled at Windsor and used to draw private carriages. Now they are used for more important royal functions. Eight Windsor Greys, harnessed in pairs and

62   Hannibal, the drum horse, being ridden by Henry Gray at the Trooping of the Colour.

▲
63 The first woman police rider – of the seventies.

Horse Guards give the royal salute as they pass Buckingham Palace. They ride black horses, except for the trumpeter, who rides a grey, and they sometimes wear red and sometimes blue tunics.

The Queen's Life Guards ride out each morning to mount the Guard at 11 am at Whitehall, and they provide sentries through the day until 4 pm, changing every hour. Traditional ceremonies such as a royal wedding, the State opening of Parliament, or the reception of a visiting Head of State are all accompanied by squadrons of Household Cavalry.

The Household Cavalry drum horses are big and impressive animals. Either skewbald or piebald, they must be strong to support the solid silver drums they carry. Their riders guide them by reins attached to the stirrup irons.

Police Horses

More than 200 horses are kept in the Metropolitan area of London. They still perform their original role of patrolling the streets and parks to keep them safe. But the police horses are most useful in their work of controlling crowds. For example, at football matches, spectators can get out of control and people are usually frightened into behaving when faced with horses charging at them.

Police horses also take part in major ceremonies, along with the Household Cavalry and the King's Troop. They are always on duty outside Buckingham Palace during the Changing of the Guard, and the Queen rides a police horse during the Trooping of the Colour.

Police horses have to be very well-trained and have good temperaments so that they remain calm in traffic and during demonstrations where things sometimes become violent. In fact, the horses undergo special "nuisance" training, so that they become used to the noise and disturbances they will

postillion-ridden, were used to draw the Gold State Coach at the Queen's coronation. The State Coach has been used at every coronation since that of George IV and is the only coach that may only proceed at the walk.

The Household Cavalry consists of a mounted squadron of the Life Guards, stabled at the Knightsbridge Barracks, and of the Royal Horse Guards, stabled at the Hyde Park Barracks. The Royal Horse Guards were nicknamed the Blues, after their blue tunics, and amalgamated with the Royal Dragoons in 1969 to become the Blues and Royals. Each morning the Royal

have to meet. The mounted forces are so well-trained that they can give displays with ease and so earn the respect of the general public by giving demonstrations of trick riding and musical rides.

Heavy Horses

The work horse, as such, faded out after the Second World War, but a few heavy horses continued to be shown and now there has been a revival in the heavy horse industry. More and more heavy horses are being entered at shows, and ploughing match organizers are re-introducing classes for horse ploughing. The Southern Counties Horse Ploughing Association has recently been established to promote and encourage horse ploughing.

There are heavy horse breed society shows held for all four breeds of heavy horses, the Shire, Clydesdale, Percheron and Suffolk Punch. The National Shire Horse Show is held at the East of England showground, Peterborough, in March each year.

In 1972 a new event for heavy horses was established, when heavy horse working demonstrations were held. These events are not

64 The Trooping of the Colour. Her Majesty the Queen inspects the guards at the Horse Guards Parade, London to mark her official birthday in June.

competitive, but give much pleasure to horsemen and spectators. The horses demonstrate cultivation in the spring and harvesting in the autumn.

Today, heavy horses are also making a comeback on the farms, being used especially for short haul work, for a horse and cart can move just as efficiently as a tractor and trailer and, for short jobs, a horse is more economical. For example, any job which entails a lot of stopping, starting, loading and unloading is easier with a horse.

Cart horses are still used for other purposes. Some breweries still employ horses to pull their drays laden with barrels of beer from their breweries to the pubs. In Aberdeen a pair of Clydesdales are now being used for delivery services as a result of the rising cost of fuel. A Clydesdale horse costs from £900 and can work for about 12 years. Harness is £2,000 or thereabouts and a cart as little as £800. Against this, a van may well cost £8,500 and will only last seven years. Of course, after all that, a van will cost more than a horse to keep on the road.

Riding for the Disabled

One recently developed use of the horse is to provide riding for the disabled. This first started in 1947 when, after an epidemic of polio, it was found that riding provided excellent therapy, and since then, in 1969, the Riding for the Disabled Association was formed and all over the country branches have been established to help and provide enjoyment for the disabled. Each group has an organizer, a riding instructor, probably a physiotherapist, and about twenty-five helpers. Usually three helpers are needed per rider, one to lead the pony and one on each

66 The pair of Clydesdales reintroduced by the City of Aberdeen Leisure and Recreation Department, at work in the winter of 1981.

side to steady the rider. In most groups ponies are lent by private owners. But some are hired from riding schools. The Duchess of Norfolk is President of the RDA and Princess Anne its patron.

Rare Breeds

Finally, rare breeds of horses and ponies can be seen at various animal centres, as well as at zoos and stately homes all over Britain. Heavy horses can also be seen at centres. Falabellas, which are miniature horses, are particularly popular. Many studs including the National Stud are often open to visitors.

Pet, Partner and Friend

So the status of the horse has changed over the centuries. Once our servant and slave, he has become over the years wholly domesticated, a part of the family — pet, partner and friend.

Date List

2000 BC	Horses and chariots used in war
1000 BC	Cavalries formed by the larger tribes
700 BC	Chariot racing introduced at the Olympic Games in Greece
55 BC	Caesar invades Britain with a cavalry force
100 AD	The invention of the horse-shoe
400s	Attila and the Huns fight the Romans
700	The invention of the stirrup
1066	William the Conqueror comes to Britain
1100s	Horses imported from France
1300s	The Crusades — horses imported from the East
1555	The coach introduced to Britain
1640s	Stage coaches invented
1660s	The Turnpike Toll System set up
1660s	Origins of Household Cavalry and Royal Horse Guards under Charles II
1704	Marlborough wins at the Battle of Blenheim
1752	Jockey Club formed The first steeplechase run in Ireland
1769	The first circus run by Astley
1776	The first St Leger
1778	The first Oaks The Official Racing Calendar first published
1780	The first Derby
1784	Mail Coaches introduced
1791	The General Stud Book established
1805	The Battle of Waterloo The Bow Street Runners formed
1814	The first 2,000 Guineas

66

1815	McAdam and Telford improve the roads
1819	The first 1,000 Guineas
1829	Shillibeer invents the omnibus
1830s	Various new vehicles introduced such as hackney cabriolets and hansom cabs
1839	The first Grand National
1842	Mines Act forbids employment of women and children in mines Introduction of pit ponies
1854	The Charge of the Light Brigade
1850s	Polo brought to England
1870s	Trams introduced in towns
1878	Formation of Shire and Clydesdale Breed Societies
1881	The Master of Foxhounds Association formed
1899-1902	The Boer War
1907	The first Royal International Horse Show
1921	FEI founded
1923	The British Show Jumping Association formed
1924	The Cheltenham Gold Cup established
1929	The Pony Club started
1956	The British Driving Society formed
1969	The Riding for the Disabled Association formed
1970	Combined Driving international competition first held
1972	Working demonstrations by cart horses first held

Glossary

Andalusian a Spanish breed of horse.

Arabian/Arab breed of horse in whose pedigree there is only Arabian blood. The Arab is the purest and most beautiful of horses.

artillery weapons of war.

barb breed originating in Morocco and Algeria.

bit part of the bridle that the horse holds in its mouth.

cantle the back part of the saddle.

cart horse a large horse suitable for drawing a cart. The four cart horses of Great Britain are the Shire, Clydesdale, Percheron and Suffolk Punch.

cavalry a troop of soldiers on horseback.

charger a war horse.

chivalry the system of knighthood in Medieval times.

Clydesdale one of the four breeds of English cart horse.

cob not a breed, but a well-established type of horse. It is a big-bodied, short-legged, hardy type suitable for riding and driving.

colt male ungelded horse up to four years of age.

courser a swift horse; the old-fashioned term for a horse used for racing.

Criollo a breed of horse of South American origin.

dressage "training the horse in obedience and manners". Dressage tests are part of one- or three-day events and are intended to show how well horse and rider work in harmony.

equitation the art of horse riding.

feather the hair covering the fetlocks of cart horses.

filly a female horse or pony up to four years of age.

gelding a castrated male horse or pony.

girth gall a rubbing of the horse's skin, caused by a hard or dirty girth.

hack not a breed, but a type — a horse or pony used for riding.

harness horse used for drawing vehicles — wagons, carts, carriages, etc.

Haute Ecole (High School) the classical art of riding originating in Italy in the 1500s and practised at the Spanish Riding School in Vienna and at the Cadre Noir, which is the French cavalry school.

hostler (ostler) one who attended to the horses when they arrived at the inn.

Lipizzaner a breed of Spanish horses. Grey ones are used in the Spanish Riding School in Vienna.

mount a horse that is used for riding rather than for driving.

Percheron one of the four breeds of English cart horse. It originally came from France.

piebald a black horse with white patches.

pommel the front part of the saddle.

postillion a man who drives a team of horses from the saddle instead of from the driving seat on the carriage.

ride to hounds to go hunting on horseback.

running geldings old-fashioned term for horses that raced.

saddle cloths cloths used on the horses' backs under the saddle.

saddle horses used for riding.

Shetland the smallest of the nine mountain and moorland breeds of Great Britain.

shire horse one of the four breeds of cart horses.

skewbald the colour of a horse or pony — brown or any other colour except black with white patches.

spurs metal heel frames with a projection for goading the horse and which are attached to boots by a leather strap.

stable management a knowledge of how to keep a horse in the stable and at grass.

stallion a male horse.

stud book one giving the pedigree of a certain breed of horse

Suffolk Punch one of the four breeds of English cart horses, originally coming from East Anglia.

thoroughbred the English breed of race horse.

track phase part of a three-day event — the horse must cover a certain distance along roads and lanes as well as jumping fences across country.

Books
for Further Reading

The Horseman's International Book of Reference
Stanley Paul & Co Ltd, 1980

Charles Chenevix-Trench,
The History of Horsemanship,
Doubleday & Co Inc, 1970

Anthony Dent (presented by),
The Horse Through 50 Centuries of Civilization,
Phaidon, 1974

John Ellis,
Cavalry The History of Mounted Warfare,
Westbridge Books, 1978

Jane Kidd,
The Book of Horses,
Albany Books, 1980

Roger Longrigg,
The English Squire and his Sport,
Michael Joseph, 1977

Josephine Pullein Thompson (compiled by),
Horses and their Owners — An Anthology,
Nelson, 1970

Sue Simmons (Ed),
The Military Horse,
Marshall Cavendish, 1976

D.J. Smith,
Discovering Horse Drawn Carriages,
Shire Horse Publications

Philip Sumner,
Carriages,
Her Majesty's Stationery Office, 1970

J.N.P. Watson,
The Book of Foxhunting,
Batsford, 1977

Index

The numbers in **bold type** refer to the figure numbers of the illustrations.